Selected poems and song lyrics
1998-2008

ROUNDHEAD PUBLICATIONS

For my wife Robina

Also by Attila the Stockbroker

BOOKS

Cautionary Tales For Dead Commuters (Unwin, 1985) sold out, deleted

Scornflakes (Bloodaxe, 1992) available

The Rat Tailed Maggot and Other Poems (Roundhead, 1998) currently sold out but will be reprinted soon

Goldstone Ghosts (football poems - Roundhead, 2001) sold out

CDs/DVD (all available)

Spirit of the Age (Roundhead, 2008)) compilation of 28 years' work, solo and with his band Barnstormer

Live In Norway (Crispin Glover, 2007) solo poems and songs

Zero Tolerance (Roundhead, 2004) with his band Barnstormer

Live In Belfast (Roundhead, 2003) solo poems and songs

Just One Life (Roundhead, 2000) with his band Barnstormer

The Siege of Shoreham (Roundhead, 1996) with his band Barnstormer

Two compilations of earlier solo material previously available on vinyl:

The Pen & The Sword – Selected Songs 1981-1999 (Roundhead, 1999)

Poems Ancient & Modern – A Live Anthology 1981-1999 (Roundhead, 1999)

DVD:

Live at the Heartland Café (2004) solo poems and songs

All these can be purchased at gigs and through Attila's website and myspace page: www.attilathestockbroker.com / www.myspace.com/attilastockbroker (click on the online shop in each case), via iTunes or from PO Box 668, Portslade, East Sussex BN42 4BG.

CDs/DVD are £11 inc p&p apart from *Spirit of the Age*, which is £6. Scornflakes book £7. Cheques to John Baine.

For booking enquiries or to contact Attila please email or write to the above address.

To join Attila's free mailing list (for gig details etc) please email attila@solutionsinc.co.uk

Foreword

It's been ten years since my last (non-football) book, I've written loads of material and after some difficult choices these are the ones I consider to be the best. As I write this I've racked up a total of 28 years as Attila the Stockbroker, and aside from a few months when I first started, I've managed to fulfil my dream - earning my living doing what I love. Writing and performing words and music, spreading ideas, standing up for the things I believe in, meeting new people, travelling the world.

No god, no master. I guess the title poem says it all...

These words were written to be performed live, either as poems or songs. If you've bought this book at a gig, you'll know that already! When I started in 1980 I armed myself with a quote from the great Adrian Mitchell: 'Most people ignore most poetry because most poetry ignores most people'. 'Poetry' has an awful reputation in some quarters, and I have devoted my adult life to trying to change that.

I have always aimed to go where most poetry doesn't – both literally and metaphorically.

You'll find me in arts centres, libraries, universities, cafés and schools of course – but more often at punky gigs in pubs and rock venues, at music festivals, squats and political demonstrations and in mainland Europe in the huge network of radical autonomous youth centres which provide such a vibrant network for performers like myself. And, of course, as Poet in Residence at my beloved Brighton & Hove Albion FC. I published a collection of my football poems in 2001 and there are one or two new ones in here...

I don't mess about. I've got lots to say, and I'm out there saying it. To those whining head-in-the-sand types who moan 'politics has got nothing to do with poetry/music/art' (delete as appropriate) I have one response. 'Politics' affects the lives of every single person on this planet. Music and words, when combined effectively, can do the same and can inspire people to take control of their lives for the better. That's where I start from. And as I turn 50 I'm hugely inspired by the fact that I see around me a new generation of young poets, songwriters and musicians who have the same fire in their bellies and desire for change and social justice as I do.

This book is for them. Keep on keeping on!

But above all it's for my wife Robina, whose love, intelligence and constant refusal to let me get away with easy thoughts and answers ('I'll always expect better from you!') drives me ever forwards. It's no coincidence that much of my best work has been written in the ten years we've known each other!

And of course there's far more to this book than activism and politics. All human, and some animal, life is here, and many of these pieces are simply about things which have happened to me. Some are very personal.

Thanks for buying it – and have fun!

Attila, March 2008

Contents

My Poetic Licence

Yo! I'm the MC of ranting rebel poetry!
I know my history and my identity
I'm independent, a red cottage industry
DIY from here to eternity...
Now let me tell you what's been going on:
I take inspiration from centuries long gone
Oral tradition of sedition, that's my position -
No court jester with a tame disposition!
Poetic licence? 28 years I've had one
And they don't come easy, they're not handed out for fun
You have to earn it, work and sweat and move -
Not get stuck in a dead poet bore groove.
I earned mine in dirty scummy punk clubs
Rock gigs, arts centres, festivals and dodgy pubs
And yes, once or twice I've had to fight -
But when a fascist hits a poet, the poet's doing something right!
So listen up, this MC's here to stay
Wild all those years ago and still fired up today
I love words and I've got this message for you:
Poetry's not boring - though some poets bore you...
And I have to say that some poets bore me.
They're about as fun as a week on the lavatory.
Dull and pretentious, playing the Art Game -
Real problem is they give the rest of us a bad name.
But I'm in the forward line, down there in the scrum.
Tedious whining poets - up your bum!
Now some of the critics think my stuff's no good
But I earn my living at it - those jerks never could...
Yes, as you see, I'm a little bit bolshy too -
But that's just one of the ways I want to get through
Sometimes it's cerebral, dry, esoteric wit
Sometimes it's loud and wild and hard and rude as shit!
I love words and I love 'em in the red and raw
I like to use them in ways they've not been used before
Want you to laugh and want you to think as well -
Bollocks to TV - this is live, as live as hell!
Oral tradition - the real origins of poetry.
Attila the Stockbroker - ranting rebel MC.
Dean of the Social Surrealist University.
Welcome to my wild poetic journey!

Asylum Seeking Daleks

They claim their planet's dying:
that soon it's going to blow
And so they're coming here - they say
they've nowhere else to go
With their strange computer voices
and their one eye on a pole
They're moving in next door and then
they're signing on the dole...

Asylum seeking Daleks
are landing here at noon!
Why can't we simply send them back
or stick them on the moon?
It says here in the Daily Mail
they're coming here to stay -
The Loony Lefties let them in!
The middle class will pay...

They say that they're not terrorists:
That doesn't wash with me!
The last time I saw one I hid
Weeks behind the settee...
Good Lord - they're pink. With purple bumps!
There's photos of them here!
Not just extra-terrestial...
The bloody things are queer!

Yes! Homosexual Daleks
And they're sponging off the State!
With huge Arts Council grants
to teach delinquents how to skate!
It's all here in the paper -
I'd better tell the wife!
For soon they will EXTERMINATE
Our British way of life...

This satire on crass ignorance
and tabloid-fostered fear
Is at an end. Now let me give
One message, loud and clear.
Golf course, shop floor or BNP:
Smash bigotry and hate!
Asylum seekers - welcome here.
You racists: emigrate!

Too Much Pressure

(Written just before my 50th birthday)

This angry young man is still angry, but older -
And now Father Time has just pissed on my shoulder.
'You've got to grow up, John - you're way past that stage!
You've reached the condition they call 'middle age'.
It's time to be quiet, say 'yes', watch TV -
High spot of the week, a nice dinner party
Polite conversation until you doze off
The topics: house prices, taxation and goff.
(That's golf, by the way, in case you're unsure -
Not pale folk in graveyards obsessed by The Cure)
Now just look at you in your Seventies gear
With your punk rock and football and microbrew beer
Political poems and loud, angry songs
You still want to change things and right the world's wrongs?
You stand up and shout and you get in a rage:
It's really not right in a man of your age.
On top of all that, and I don't mean to frighten -
Worst of all for your blood pressure: you support Brighton!
They're not very good and you don't want to die
So sit on the couch and watch Chelsea on Sky...'

NO!!!!!!!!!!!!!!!!!

Sure, I'll take the tablets, and drink a bit less.
If you fancy a game, I might play you at chess.
I hope that I'll make it till I'm ninety-five.
But one thing's for sure, Death - you'll take me alive!

Supermodel

Prepubescent imagery.
Empty, stupid eyes.
Waif thin.
Tyrannical.
No fat.
No body hair.
No character, no love, no personality -
no brain.
So thin, and yet...
so thick.
By your anodyne complicity
in this gruesome stereotype
you connive
in the corporate enslavement of your sisters
- anorexia, bulimia, self-loathing, fear.
They aspire to be like you
- an unnatural creation of capital -
and wreck their bodies in the process,
destroy their fertility,
tear apart their lives.
But hang on a minute?
Not my place to talk about that?
I'm a man, what do I know?
You're just trying to earn a living?
What I'm saying has been said before?
OK.
But when the football blokes look
and make some expected remark
I'm supposed to join in.
I'm supposed to fancy you -
or pretend to.
Well, I don't.
And I won't.
More than that.
You revolt me.
You give me an inversion.
It's quite simple really.
I just don't desire a stupid adman's toy
styled to look like a prepubescent girl

- a real 'babe' -
there in the tabloid
next to the lurid description
of Gary Glitter's downfall.
I love a real woman.

I won't buy the product you advertise.
I won't watch your latest film.
I'm not interested in your poxy TV series
I'll never set foot in that fucking car
and I hate you.
I know I should just ignore you, or feel sorry for you
but I hate you
and your fashionist masters
bringers of misery
destroyers of individuality
harbingers of despair.
Women and men:
Riot against diet!
Sod the microchip revolution -
let's have a fish 'n' chip one!
Cream bun chocolate cream bun chocolate
lard lard sag aloo beer beer beer!
Riot against diet!
Smash fashionism!
Say goodbye to Hello!
Make Cosmopolitan....cosmopolitan!
Let's have a real Woman's Realm!
Take over the curry house
Fill your freezer full of ice cream
Live
Love
Get real!

Poison Pensioner

I've tried to work it out but I just can't see
How a cretin like you is related to me
You've just one brain cell and that one's a mess
Parroting rubbish from the Daily Express
No, not the Sun: you'd say that was a 'rag'
Delusions of grandeur from a jumped up hag
But don't get ideas: you're as thick as a shoe
Poison Pensioner - this poem's for you

I've had it up to here and I'm cutting up rough
Distant relative? Not distant enough!
Ever thought of space travel, prejudiced cow?
I'd suggest Uranus but you're up there right now
You've a monochrome vision of a world that's dead
A million Reader's Digests inside your head
I'd like to put vomit in your cheese fondue
Poison Pensioner - this poem's for you

You worked all your life in the public sector
And all you ever did was whine and hector
Moan about the people who fought your cause
Cheer for the Tories and their union laws
You were born in a council house, you clueless bitch
But you side with the Right and you vote with the rich
Bowing and scraping to the privileged few
Poison Pensioner - this poem's for you

You've a medal for meddling, that's for sure
If this was my house then I'd show you the door
But my mum needs help and you're here to see her
So I sit and listen to your verbal gonorrhea
Right now I wish I was in her head
'Cos Mum won't remember a word you've said
Your compassionate act just got a bad review
Poison Pensioner - this poem's for you

Bossy yet servile, some combination!
Paralysed spine of a lickspittle nation
Could have been a builder, ended up a tool
Lifelong victim of divide and rule
You're a Ragged Trousered Philanthropist
Who wasn't even waiting for the boat you've missed
You're a turkey voting for Christmas too
Poison Pensioner - this poem's for you

Use of English

(A poem about one of the Poison Pensioner's favourite expressions!)

The phrase 'politically correct'
Is not at all what you'd expect.
But how has it been hijacked so?
I'm going to tell you, 'cos I know.

You'd think it should mean kind and smart
Radical and stout of heart
A way of living decently.
Well, so it did, till recently.

And then some cringing, nerdy divs
Sweaty, misogynistic spivs
Sad, halitosis-ridden hacks
All wearing lager-stained old macs
With spots and pustules and split ends
And absolutely zero friends
(Yes, living, breathing running sores:
The right wing press's abject whores)
Were all told, by their corporate chiefs
To rubbish decent folks' beliefs
To label with the phrase 'PC'
All that makes sense to you and me
And write off our progressive past.
Their articles came thick and fast
The editors gladly received them
And loads of idiots believed them.

You'll find that most who use the term
Will only do so to affirm
Sad, bigoted, outdated views
They've swallowed via the Murdoch news.

Oh for the days when Spam was just a Monty Python sketch

Thanks to the internet
my wife is a very happy woman.
My penis is now forty-seven feet long
it stays erect for weeks at a time
and is garlanded by hundreds of genuine Rolex watches
acquired with the millions I have won
in various Albanian lotteries
and the billions generously deposited in my accounts
by the grateful executors of the wills
of innumerable African tribal chiefs
all mysteriously deceased
along with their entire extended families
in improbably gruesome lawnmower accidents in Liechtenstein.
My account with Lloyds has been suspended.
(I don't have one.)
My wife's breasts
enlarge and reduce, spontaneously,
as we use our 95% discounted software
to gaze at the pictures of our free timeshare apartments
enjoying continuous multiple orgasms
whilst admiring our genuine Chinese historical artefacts
purchased online from Hong Kong.
Our garden is full of imported rubber.
Not rubber sex toys
or even rubber boots
just: rubber.
I have more free Coldplay MP3s
than you could wave a suicide note at.
I also have Kate Moss Suction Power.
I don't know what that is,
but I am hoping it may be useful
next time the toilet needs unblocking.
I now know the Cyrillic alphabet
and the Polish for
'Are you embarrassed about your size?'

Every morning, a new surrealist word juxtaposition
appears in my inbox
as the spammers seek to avoid the filter.
Applicator fornicate!
Crabmeat be Paris!
Gash ineptitude!
Out evoke in robins!
Consonant clitoris!
Bestiality service charge!
Decomposing lark's vomit engulf Crystal Palace!
(ok, I made the last one up,
but the others are all genuine.)
And, to prove that truth is indeed stranger than fiction
in our brave new world,
my website is recommended
as one of the top fifty stockbroking sites
on many search engines.

Now that really IS Pythonesque.

The Social Surrealist
Weapons Inspector's Report

I am one of a team
of social surrealist weapons inspectors
currently travelling through the United Kingdom
under very difficult conditions
searching for weapons of mass distraction.
The government
have denied that they exist
or have ever existed
or indeed that there is or could ever have been any reason
for New Labour to seek to distract the masses in the first place
and they have compiled an extensive dossier
of long-abandoned Labour Party achievements
as proof of their honesty, good intentions and political credibility.
These include:
creating a temporary Welfare State
nationalising the mines and railways
for a few years
reducing working hours and increasing workers' wages
a bit
and opposing the worst excesses of capitalism
from time to time
for a couple of months
in 1954
as long as it was alright with the CBI.
But a cursory glance round Britain
has uncovered hundreds of such weapons of mass destraction -
Big Brother
Pop Idol
endless meaningless 'celebrities'
The Sun 'newspaper'
and the Royal Family
to name but a few -
and our demands that they should be destroyed
in order to combat national supine gullibility
have met with strenuous opposition
not just from the government
but from a substantial number of private individuals

who scream incoherent and violent abuse
at anybody who seeks to remove these weapons
unquestioningly accept their lot
as part of the least healthy, worst educated and worst paid population
in Western Europe
and energetically defend their right to be exploited and lied to
by abject American government stooges
masquerading as the British Labour Party.

This proves not just the existence
but the supreme effectiveness
of the weapons of mass distraction
currently being employed by Mr Brown and his cronies.
We demand immediate action by the United Nations
in the form of strict sanctions
on fifth rate, lowest common denominator television programmes
and newspapers
and especially on the use of the phrase 'politically correct'
to attack anyone who isn't a right wing
misogynistic
bigoted
cretin
with the reflective powers of a lobotomised stoat.
We are, of course, working for British Intelligence -

we don't think there's enough of it about.

Punk Night at The Duck's Nuts

(A true story)

It's a Wednesday night
in Newcastle, New South Wales.
There's a pub right next to our hotel
called 'The Duck's Nuts.'
(To emphasise the point,
next to the entrance
there's a large mural of a duck on a surfboard
with his testicles hanging out.
Yes, I know ducks don't have nuts.
But this one has.
I can see them.)

I can't believe it.
'Hey, Mick' I say,
'I can't believe it!
There's a pub right next to our hotel
called 'The Duck's Nuts!'
And look at this mural!'
Mick's not really surprised at all.
He explains that in Australian
to say something is 'the duck's nuts'
means you think it's really, really good.
That figures, I guess.
In England, if we think something's really, really good
we say it's 'the dog's bollocks' -
at least my friends and I do.
I doubt if the Queen does.
Nevertheless, I am still surprised
because to the best of my knowledge
we don't have any pubs in England called 'The Dog's Bollocks'
nor any pub signs which feature dogs' testicles
- though it's true that we do have a beer of that name.
Typical English understatement,
I suppose.

Anyway, Mick and I have just done a gig
at Newcastle University
supporting a very famous Aussie band called the Whitlams
who sound like Supertramp on Mogadon.
We've escaped
it's past midnight
and a beer or two at The Duck's Nuts
seems like a very good idea.

But there's no Dog's Bollocks at the Duck's Nuts -
in fact, nothing even remotely drinkable
for a real ale fan like myself -
and the lager I am handed is unspeakable:
the hamster's bladder contents and then some.
There is a punk band playing in the corner.
The guitarist has spiky hair and a broken hand.
They are playing Green Day covers very loudly
and after the Whitlams, they sound absolutely bloody fantastic to me.
There are about twenty people in the pub
all of whom are over sixty
all of whom are very pissed.
To be the youngest person at a gig
isn't something that happens to me much these days -
but it hardly seems to matter.

The audience
- if one can call them an audience -
is staring at the band.
They obviously don't think they are the duck's nuts
or the dog's bollocks
or even the lemming's gonads
because they don't applaud
at the end of the songs
they just drink, stare into space
and get even more pissed
- which is very pissed indeed.

We applaud.
We're musicians.
We sympathise.
And anyway I think they're pretty good
(for a Green Day covers band...)

Suddenly they stop playing
and announce that they're having a break.
A break?
It's one o'clock in the morning
and they're stopping for a break?
Yes, they've got to do two more sets -
in the middle of the night
to twenty semi-comatose pensioners
who by now are completely oblivious to their surroundings.

I think of the worst gigs I have ever done.
There is no contest.
I have seen Hell.

Jean Paul Sartre wasn't specific enough.
Hell is not other people.
Hell is three sets
between midnight and 3am
to twenty elderly alcoholics
in a testicular theme pub
on a Wednesday night
in Newcastle, New South Wales.

Punk night at the Duck's Nuts.

Inspired by a headline on the billboard for our local newspaper...

Shed Fire

A perfect English pageantry:
an act so gloriously mundane
New neighbours put up eight foot fence
So strangers now will thus remain
As English as our small town press
who'd like so much to dish the dirt
but headline uneventfulness:
'Local shed fire. No-one hurt.'

A cod war veteran complains
about some kids skateboarding by
The Daily Mail sells very well
And he and it see eye to eye
The homeless sleep under the pier
But most round here don't seem to care
That's city life, another's news.
Shed fire, though. Police aware.

The poster shouts it, black and white
A headline story, that's for sure
And there's a pull out TV guide
For folk who rarely ask for more
And two, more lively than the rest,
Are chatting in the autumn sun.
Not in their back yard, thank god,
But: shed fire. Little damage done.

Frogspawn Man versus the Boy Racers

(another true story)

Mid nineties.
March.
West Sussex.
I've been to a stream
next to the A27
looking for frogspawn
to populate our brand new garden pond.
I guess I first went there when I was about seven
and have been many times since.
The road is much wider now
the cars are faster
and most of the stream is gone
but one stubborn bit remains
next to the concrete and the cars
and the frogs have obviously had
an orgy of Bacchanalian proportions.
I've found lots of spawn, very quickly.
A glutinous, black-specked mess
fills my bucket.
It's a beautiful spring day.
I'm very happy
full of memories of my father
seven years old again.
I stand by the side of the road
next to the traffic lights
and wait for my lift home.

Suddenly I realise
that an inarticulate-sounding man in his mid twenties
in some kind of penis extension car
has wound down his window
and is shouting abuse at me.
The lights change -
the glans glides off.
Then another man makes a two fingered gesture at me.
A car full of techno nerds
turns down the techno
and hurls a collective t-t-t-techno insult.
The next time the light goes red
a middle aged, middle class Southwick zip up jumper husband
in a middle aged, middle class Southwick zip up jumper car
draws up beside me
and glares at me with undisguised contempt.

He looks as though he would like to shout something
but no-one from Southwick talks to strangers
let alone shouts at them
so he just glares at me.

I stare back.
I don't glare.
I just stare.
I am very puzzled.

I check my person.
I am fully clothed.
My flies are done up.
My mud spattered T-shirt bears the logo
of an obscure folk band from Wigan.
Does everyone really hate the Tansads that much?

I am totally confused.
It's a beautiful Spring day
I am standing by the traffic lights
on a West Sussex A road
holding a bucket of frogspawn
and suddenly everybody hates me!
Another car hurtles past -
occupants screaming abuse.

Then the lights change again.
A car draws up beside me.
A very flash, shiny one.
The boy racer inside is shaking his head.
He is gesturing to me
as though I am about to do something totally unacceptable
to something very important to him
and he really doesn't want me to.
I stand there.
I gaze at him in absolute bewilderment.

His window opens.
Then his mouth.
'Bloody squeegee merchant. Don't you touch my fucking car.
Piss off and get a fucking job!'

I look at him in astonishment.
What has he just said?

Then the penny drops.
I am standing by the traffic lights.
I am holding a bucket.
He thinks I am about to start cleaning his car windscreen
without his permission.

I walk over to the car.
I tip the bucket up slightly
and proffer the contents to him.
It is his turn to be confused.
He's a boy racer.
His car has a Romford dealership sticker on the window
He doesn't exactly have a herpetologist's soul.
He stares at the contents of my bucket.
He doesn't know what it is.
However, I think he realises that I'm not going to start
cleaning his windscreen with it.

The lights change
he roars off
I walk back to the side of the road
and laugh till the tears run down my cheeks
till my sides are killing me
till I pull a muscle.

—⁓—

It's March
eight years later.
Our pond is full of spawn -
the great grandtadpoles of that original bucketful.
As I crouch to look at the developing specks
the memory comes back.
I start to shake
the tears run down my cheeks
I nearly overbalance into the pond.
I run inside
I write this poem
I feel so happy.

On being 'European'

A while ago, I received this email

Dear Attila the Stockbroker

We are in the process of compiling a handbook of anecdotes, views and observations which have shaped the thinking and attitudes of a wide range of people with regard to the UK's relationship with Europe, supported by easily understandable factual and historical information. Our primary objective is to publish an honest and interesting book for the widest possible readership, to assist in a more informed debate as the development of the European Union unfolds. We have no political affiliations and no axe to grind; our motivations are simply to inform the general public, and assist in the improvement of the debate, whatever the results may be. With all this in mind, we write to ask if you might be willing to contribute a written piece which best reflects your feelings regarding the UK's relationship with Europe, whatever they may be.

Yours, Tom & Simon Sykes

I have been asked to give my thoughts on the UK's relationship with Europe. I have always been astonished how the question arises. It's like asking me about my relationship with my arm.

There are six continents. Asia, America, Antarctica, Australia, Africa and Europe.

The UK isn't in any of the other five, is it, UK Alcohol Dependence Party? Is it, Daily Mail, Express, Sun reading amoeba heads? Did you DO geography at school? Inger-land, Blighty, The Old Country, whatever, depending on your social background and chosen form of address (and England is the only bit you actually care about, isn't it?) is in YUR-OP. We - that's all of us, are indisputably, implacably EUROPEAN!

We are. And there is absolutely nothing you can do about it. The only kind of relationship the UK has with Europe is the kind you have with that lager-filled beer gut of yours, or your gout, or the nasty disease you caught from your butler, or if you're a true member of the aristocracy, a member of your close family. We are part of Europe, as they are part of you. You might not like it...but we are!!

That's right. When your single functioning brain cell is finally switched on, you will eventually realise that this country is as much a part of Europe as France, Liechtenstein or any other of those strange places where the inhabitants speak a language which you don't understand! We are European. Like every other country in Europe. One among many. Not special. Got it? The only way we are special is that we're the only country in Europe where 90% of the population can't speak a foreign language....

As for the EU: I am for a European Union of the people. I am against a Europe dominated by slimy pinstriped capitalist scum. But then, I'm against a world dominated by slimy capitalist scum, and it most certainly is right now. So, in the same way that the UK isn't a special case in Europe, Europe isn't a special case in the world.

On that basis I LOVE the EU and ADORE the Euro. Why? Because they wind up xenophobic, barathea blazer wearing, chip guzzling, knotted handkerchief brandishing, 'isn't it hot?' complaining, Bernard Manning loving, PC as a term of abuse employing, football as an excuse for right wing violence using IDIOTS!

Ban the pound! Abolish the English Channel! Superglue the UK to France, right in the middle of the garlic growing region! NOW!!!!!

New World Order Rap

Change the names and fudge the dates
For United Nations read United States
They're coming soon over your border
One World Nightmare - New World Order...

Yes, they talk of Jesus Christ: Self Righteous Brothers all
And every television screen is at their beck and call
So here's a public service broadcast: he who lives, obeys
and the moral of this story is just what the dollar says...

There's no debate, there's just G8 and a global mafia superstate
Policed by thugs, awash with drugs
and kept in place by Murdoch's mugs
And Sheriff USA is there to turn you into fries
Yes you can bank on a Yank in a tank cos he who argues, dies!

Change the names and fudge the dates
For United Nations read United States
They're coming soon over your border
One World Nightmare - New World Order...

If you try to play the game you're sure to get it wrong
'cos the New World Order makes the rules up as it goes along
One minute you're its bosom pal and general factotum
The next its high technology is aimed straight at your ...head

Said sell you arms, said bomb you flat.
Said sell you arms, said bomb you flat.
Said sell you arms, then bomb you flat.
Then sell you more arms...fancy that!
You want to join another gang?
Hey look, your country just went bang!

Change the names and fudge the dates
For United Nations read United States
Fundamentalists were their friends
Are they still? Well, that depends...

Al Quaeda - now they'll bleed ya!
You'll end up just like roast pork.
They paid you to murder kids
in Commie countries, not New York!

Hey Assad, you made 'em mad
Lockerbie bomb was really bad
But now they want you on their side
So they'll forget the ones who died

Hey Saddam, time for bam-bam
They backed you against Iran
But Saudi oil is looking dodgy.
So they're gonna waste ya, podgy!

Change the names and fudge the dates
For United Nations read United States...
They're coming soon over the border
One World Nightmare - New World Order...

Hail Humanitarian Nato - that's not a bomb, it's a potato!
Just behave or dig your grave: they've got some refugees to save
It's pick and choose, some win, some lose - yes, they're in Kosovo
But Palestine, Timor, Rwanda, sorry, man, no go
Hey, it's not that they don't care,
but there aren't points to score down there
The message is to Moscow, large -
shut up and put up, they're in charge
And they don't want to lose contacts
for banking loans and arms contracts
For every psychopath they bomb
there are two more they buy stuff from
And sell stuff to and arm and train and arm again and arm again

Said arm again - said Armageddon
Said arm again - said Armageddon
Said evil thug - said trusted friend
said evil thug - said trusted friend...

Change the names and fudge the dates
For United Nations read United States
for NATO read the Pentagon
They rule the world: the reds are gone

Now Mary had a little lamb: its fleece was white as snow
But when the CIA found out, that lamb was sure to go
There WAS a Grand Old Duke of York, he HAD ten thousand men
But the New World Order carpet bombed them till he had just ten
And then they signed a big arms deal - now he's got lots again...
The Serbs the Serbs have funny verbs
and don't use vowels in their words!

Change the names and fudge the dates
For United Nations read United States
Said G8, IMF, World Bank.
Put a fascist in your tank.
Get a loan, then starve the poor -
Then they'll let you have some more.
That's the way the world is run.
Gorbachev - what have you done?

April Fool in September

All in vain.
A total waste of everything.
You'll never know - that's the point.
You'll never, ever know.
Because you killed yourselves, and all those people,
and that was that.
Quite literally, for you and for them,
end of story.
All in vain.
Your mothers' pain in childbirth,
the love of your families,
your growth, your education,
a complete waste of time.
The transition, if you want to call it that
From soft-handed sons of bourgeois parents
to your new way:
born of rage
rage at the filthy injustices perpetrated on your people
by the money thugs of the West
rage which thirty years before would have led you to
the bright red banner with the hammer and sickle of hope
to the Soviet Union and its training camps
to Marx, to Lenin, to the global liberation movements
but which now led you to...
nothing.
Conviction, conversion,
prostration before your 'god',
decision, training -
then those final few days.
Your last savourings of whatever it was in life you loved the most.
The touch of a woman, perhaps?
Although somehow I doubt that:
You hated women, didn't you -
One of you went as far as to leave instructions
that no woman should ever visit his grave...
Your last drink. Your last meal.
The unbearable tension as you went through the checks.
Then the elation of success, control, power!
All for nothing.
Brutality on board,
slashing, beating:
the beseeching, cringing victims
phoning their loved ones
for the very last time

and then the moment
when you approached
those sterile momuments to Mammon
full of living human beings
many of them poorer and more screwed down by the money power
than you had ever been
bared your chests, welcomed your 'god'-
and then you found out.
Or rather, you didn't.
You just died.
Your tissue, your existence immolated in one split second
And then - oblivion.
The indescribable nightness of not being.
No Paradise, no life after death,
No martyrs, no holy war, nothing.
Just oblivion...
and the sobs of the bereaved.

Now I go back.
Back to Gorbachev, cringing before capital.
Back to the people dancing on the Berlin Wall,
then crashing off, to find no safety net below,
just the merciless sneers of the usurer.
Back to the day the poor, the oppressed, the brutalised of the world
were told
'The Red Flag has been lowered!
MacSociety has won!
Welcome to the New World Order!'
Justice hungry people left without Marx's standard
and a Western backed spawn of clerics
there to fill the void
and twist the minds of a generation of dupes
into the walking bombs of today
- walking into nothing.
Hey, America!
In the 80s you armed them in Afghanistan.
In the 90s you armed them in Bosnia.
Now they fly to your citadel
and bite the hand that feeds.
April Fool, America!
April Fool, Islamic 'martyr!'
April Fool in September.
April Fool.

Crime Writer

Who's the killer, the bigger killer?
Who is ill and who is iller?
Who's the killer, the bigger killer?
Here's a tale from MC Attila

White estate, some newtown overspill
Kind of place where life's always uphill
They know the score, same shit, same dice to roll
Football, boxing, music or the dole
Some rise up and shine, some burn and die
Most look out for the best way to get by
One just can't find any way at all
Blank eyes stare at a dead end brick wall

Who's the killer, the bigger killer?
Who is ill and who is iller?
Who's the killer, the bigger killer?
Here's a tale from MC Attila

Back from a two hour full-on liquid lunch
London journo lines up another punch
People he's not met, places he's never been
Soft targets for his hack spleen
Immigrants of course, at number one
Endless stories, endless source of fun
Two men, two worlds, both men dead inside...
One more man then we'll watch three worlds collide...

Who's the killer, the bigger killer?
Who is ill and who is iller?
Who's the killer, the bigger killer?
Hear this tale from MC Attila

Third man comes from somewhere far away
Thought with prayers and love he'd be OK
Prayers and love stopped when the wars began
Fled with his family, as would any man
Two long years they had to run and roam
Wept with joy when they got their new home
Run down flat in newtown white estate
Near someone with too much time to hate...

Who's the killer, the bigger killer?
Who is ill and who is iller?
Who's the killer, the bigger killer?
Hear this tale from MC Attila

Hack's in the pub as the presses start to roll
Headline screams 'Asylum on the dole!'
Yes, more tired and cliché ridden crap
Just enough to make a strung out string snap
Blank eyes stare at the tabloid's front page
Kicks the wall in dumb, frustrated rage
Heads for home and grabs a petrol can
Then goes hunting for his fellow man...

Who's the killer, the bigger killer?
Who is ill and who is iller?
Who's the killer, the bigger killer?
That's the question from MC Attila

Awful screams as the murder flames bite
Horror strikes and death lights up the night
Blank eyes picked up the very next day
Hack's there at his desk, tapping away
'Lock him up and throw away the key!'
Wallows in his foul hypocrisy
Who's most to blame for this evil deed?
He who acts or he who sows the seed?

Who's the killer, the bigger killer?
Who is ill and who is iller?
Who's the killer, the bigger killer?
Make your choice...
says MC Attila

Following Joe Strummer's sad demise everyone seems to be dying at the moment - and I don't mean Maurice Gibb. You wouldn't know it from the total lack of media coverage, but Mickey Finn, Marc Bolan's bongo playing sidekick in the mighty T.Rex, died the same day as Gibb, Jan 12, 2003, at the age of 56. Although this sad event was, totally unjustly in my view, more or less ignored in the UK - sure, Mickey couldn't sing or play the bongoes very well, but he looked good on stage and was very much a part of T.Rex - this was not the case everywhere in the world.

Many former UK rock legends, forgotten in their own country, have huge followings in Japan and other countries of the Far East, and although this is not common knowledge, Mickey Finn had his own Far Eastern following....though his was rather different...!

North Korea Mourns Comrade Mickey Finn Of T.Rex

It is with unfathomable sadness and regret that the Dear Leader, Comrade Kim Jong Il, the Central Committee of the Korean Workers' Party, the regional organisations, the progressive women and youth and all the labouring masses throughout the Democratic People's Republic of Korea learned of the death of Comrade Mickey Finn, much-loved bongo player with T.Rex and beloved bongo teacher and percussive mentor to the revolutionary people of our Republic.

When the unbearable news of Comrade Mickey's untimely death reached the ears of the Korean people, spontaneous mass demonstrations broke out all over the homeland. Millions of workers, peasants and intellectuals immediately took to the streets in a huge show of proletarian love for Comrade Mickey, and the sound of bongoes being played slightly out of time rang out across all corners of the Republic. Above this occasionally erratic percussive clamour could clearly be heard the progressive slogans spontaneously rising from the lips of the people:

Glory to the immortal memory of Comrade Mickey Finn of T.Rex, through his much-loved recordings beloved bongo-playing tutor to Comrade Kim Il Sung, the Great Leader and his son Comrade Kim Jong-Il, the Dear Leader!

Long live the revolutionary and percussive Juche spirit embodied and reflected in the sound of Comrade Mickey's bongoes!

Death to the American imperialists and their British lackeys who dare
to issue threats against the progressive and revolutionary nuclear
weapons programme of the DPRK and conspire to spread lies about
the homeland! Death to their filthy media running dogs who ignore
the life and work of Comrade Mickey Finn!

Glory to his bongoes! Glory to authentically produced percussive
sound! Death to electronically-produced and computer-generated so
called 'dance music!' Let us take new initiatives in the field of culture
to honour the memory of Comrade Mickey!

Let us make it clear to the progressive peoples of the world that
'house music' lives in the house of the bourgeoisie,
and 'trance' is the state of mind of those
who have been fooled by the lies of the U.S imperialists
and their lackeys!

Let us ensure that henceforth the only 'techno'
in revolutionary Korea is the ever greater techno-logical development
of our militant and steel-like response to all aggressors:
PEOPLE'S REVOLUTIONARY NUCLEAR WAR!

That the only 'deep house'
is the radiation-proof underground bunker of the Dear Leader,
Comrade Kim Jong-Il!

That the only 'garage'
is the silo system housing the launchers for our militant revolutionary
people's inter-continental nuclear ballistic missiles!

That the only 'acid house'
is the interrogation chamber reserved for all internal
anti-Party elements!

That the only 'chill-out zone'
is the mortuary, destination of all those who dare to raise their hands
against the revolutionary Korean people!

That 'Old Skool'
means but one thing -
the immortal teachings of Marx, Engels, Lenin...

AND STALIN!

Dialectical Materialism, T.Rex and the Chinese

As we know,
Karl Marx
used Hegelian philosophy
as the basis of his
dialectical materialism -
a way of
analysing human behaviour
and explaining history.
It's not easy to understand.
Bloody hard going in fact.
Part of the dialectic
involves the theory of the unity of opposites.
I had real problems with that.
Aged about fourteen
I recall struggling with Marx's
'Grundrisse der politischen Ökonomie'
while listening to 'Electric Warrior' by T.Rex.
As far as language was concerned,
I distinctly remember finding Marc's
rather less taxing than Marx.
But I do know I never got the two mixed up.

Unlike me,
the new General Secretary of the Chinese Communist Party
must have completely understood Marx's theory
of the unity of opposites.
In fact, he positively defined it not long ago
when at the recent Communist Party Congress
he invited capitalists to join.

(And lots and lots must have done..
judging by the way they stitched up Rover...)

I think he must have listened to T.Rex too.
He's one of the Children of the Revolution.
And on the Chinese Road to Socialism
He's driving a Rolls Royce -
'cos it's good for his voice,
of course.

Two Glastonbury Errors

(Dedicated to the memory of Arabella Churchill)

Now I've performed at Glastonbury since 1982 –
That's 22 so far I think, though each year feels like new
I've seen it grow from hippy roots into a massive splurge
You get the lot, from ranting poets to quids-in corporate dirge
And that's OK. Each to their own. Us old school hardcore purists
And all the mobile-cashpoint-weekend-hippie Glasto tourists.
I have a thousand memories of sunshine, rain and flood!
Joe Strummer on the main stage, John Peel in the mud...
No time for all. Two special stories: they're a rare old mixture.
The beer-befuddled memoirs of a punk rock Glasto fixture.

The first concerns a gruesome and apocryphal event
Concerning those unfortunates ensconced in the Dance Tent
One afternoon when Glasto staff were cleaning out the loos.
The bloke inside the toilet truck had two buttons to choose –
The one emblazoned 'Suck' and the other labelled 'Blow'...
Wrong button, wrong place and wrong time. The end result?
Oh, no.

The second is more personal and close to home, I'd say.
My wife and I were wandering one sunny Saturday
Amidst the close-pressed masses of a modern Glasto crowd
When she had a whim to do something to make her husband proud
Give me a lift, despite my beers, and really set me up
So she gently reached behind herself to make a loving cup
But my stopping by the beer tent quite undid her wifely plan
And the loving cup was given to an unsuspecting man...
Her fingers knew at once the heinous nature of her error
And she dashed off in embarrassment, confusion, pain and terror!
I've never asked Robina if the grounds for her surprise
Were because her chosen target was over- or undersized...
Or was it just a different shape? Well, that's as it may be.
Long live Michel Eavis, and long live Glastonbury!

Effineff

Poo bum willy, my name is Effineff
When you hear my shit it's time to go deaf
One more overripe press hype stereotype
Unhappy in his nappy and in need of a quick wipe
Another sad boy spewing violent, woman-hating shite
But the media love me and it's cos I'm white
And from the US - they think I'm credible
But I'm not made of chocolate so I'm not edible
And that's a real pity cos if somebody ate me
MC Attila wouldn't need to hate me

(Spice Girls section...)

But I'll tell you that I'm hard
yeah I'm really really hard
yeah I'm really really hard
yeah I'm really really really hard

If you wanna buy my records
You're about nine years old
You like lots of swearing
and consume what you are told

(So I'll tell you that I'm hard...)

Yo! Effineff, now tell us the truth!

Cardboard cut out Tarantino meets Wham!
Endless crap about how fucked up I am.
Fifth rate video nasty Cobain
Whining into some gullible kid's brain
No Rebel MC or Grandmaster Flash -
I talk hatred for heaps and heaps of cash
I'm just the ho' of a big corporation
Taking pocket money from a soap-sodden nation
Voice of youth? Oh don't take the piss!
A fillet of cod has more guts than this...

(But I'll tell you that I'm hard...)

If you wanna buy my records
you read the NME
live somewhere in Surrey
and want street credibility

(So I'll tell you that I'm hard...)

Yo! Effineff, it's past your bedtime!

Before I go I've got one more thing to say
I sum up the state of the scene today
Bland and tedious mainstream corporate shite
All controlled by the mainstream corporate Right
Kids who think 'radical' means dumb misogynistic rap
or sterile MTV crap.
Radio plays a slick processed sound
Punk never happened: no one wants to be underground
Bog standard bloated barren big business bore
It's official folks - we're back in 1974...

and I'm YES!

(But I'll tell you that I'm hard....)

That's the problem.
Here's the solution.
Another huge grass roots music revolution.
MC Attila is telling me how...
Eff off Effineff and eff off NOW!

Carriage H

(for Richard Castle)

Not the normal victims -
not this time.
Not the forgotten people:
the ones who put you there,
ground down now as before,
eighteen years of misery,
countless more of betrayal.
Theirs is a routine, everyday suffering.
You're used to that:
hospital waiting list, neighbourhood terror,
fuel poverty, the usual things.
You know how to deal with them.
They are sent to a spin doctor
and forgotten, along with their votes:
after all, you say,
they've nowhere else to go...
But it wasn't them.
Not this time.
An unusually comprehensive capitulation
to the moneylenders in the temple
even by your nice, Middle England, church-on-Sunday-and-shit-on-
thy-neighbour
'modernising' ecumenical standards, Mr. Blair.
This time, your friends connived
in the murder of some of their own -
for, yes, it was a first class inferno
in Carriage H.
And though safety before profit
and renationalisation without compensation
would bring a belly cheer of relief and hope
from everyone who entrusts their living bodies
to these everyday cylinders on wheels
and such a measure
would be one of the most popular governmental decisions
in British political history
you remain loyal.
Loyal as the puppet to the hand.
Loyal to the faceless, murderous thugs of capital

who lurk behind every New Labour smile.
The IMF. The City. The banks.
You don't care about us.
You dance on the graves of the Paddington dead
with talk of tube privatisation
and air traffic control privatisation
- the vapid sheep say nothing
and those who speak the truth
are called extremists.
And even after Hatfield and Potters Bar
when the country is crying out for justice
when police want to prosecute
the filthy profiteering scum
who murder our people
you do nothing.
My kind of Labour government
would renationalise the railways without compensation
imprison the entire board of Railtrack
and try them,
not for corporate manslaughter,
but for crimes agains the people,
reopen the Northwich salt mines
and send them to slave there for life
with loop tapes of Phil Collins' greatest hits
and slow motion videos of Crystal Palace reserve games
as their only respite.
You are not my kind of Labour government.
I want something else.
And I want it now.

On Being Defrosted

'It needs defrosting, love, and quickly too.
My husband bought it half an hour ago
Expecting that this lump of icebound flesh
Would be our lunch - he hasn't got a clue.
I said it was a foolish thing to buy.
I told him that you have a microwave.
Shame-faced, he drove me over in the car.
It needs defrosting, love, and so do I!'

The chicken frozen, you all wet and hot.
It took a while - you, thirty seconds flat.
But still, your wifely duties weren't ignored.
Your (ex) husband got dinner on the dot....
I'll buy our chickens fresh, and cook for you.
But yes, the recipe will stay the same
as on that Sunday morning lost in time.
While dinner's cooking, we'll be cooking too.

A Nasal Appraisal

(For my Darling Wife, Xmas 2001)

I love your Nose
Your Nose I kiss
I know it's not
Your Clitoris
I love your Nose
It's on your Face
Your Clit is in
A Different Place
I love your Nose
I'm glad it's There
And not among
Your Pubic Hair
I love your Nose
Its Bogies Fine
And when you're Pissed
They taste of Wine!

I love your Nose
I say with Candour
I love its Splendour
I love its Grandeur
Here is the Truth
Without Conjecture
I love Your Nasal
Architecture!
Your Steel Eyes Shine
Your Nostrils Flare
I catch a glimpse
Of Nasal Hair
And When You Sneeze
I'm On My Knees....
I love your Nose!
I love your Nose!

I love your Nose
Seat of my Lust
It's listed by
The National Trust
I love your Nose
It Fuels my Fire
A Sturdy Oak
A Mighty Spire
A Profile Fine
Chiselled in Stone
Face like a Queen
Nose like a Throne
And when it Bleeds
They know -
in Leeds....
I love your Nose!
I love your Nose!

Keeping Up Appearances

(Commissioned for Radio Four's 'Off The Page')

I come from a Keeping Up Appearances family, no doubt of that -
though my mum, bless her, is far more lovable than that awful Bucket
woman and my parents were definitely rather more understated in
their social climbing mission.
Like so much in life, of course, it was a generational thing,
especially for my much older dad, born in 1899. Both my parents
grew up in council houses with 'artisan' (to use Mum's word) fathers
- one a printer, the other an upholsterer - both left school at a young
age and, like so many of their era, both were determined to get as far
from their roots as possible. Since the printers' trade was to be
destroyed by Rupert Murdoch and upholsterers rendered obsolete by
the likes of yuppie gods Ikea, you'd have thought their class-
consciousness might have turned them into militants, proud of their
heritage. Sadly for my street credibility in the likes of the NME a
generation later, it didn't!
Hey, punk rockers. Hey, wannabe music journalists, militant
Leftists, anti fascist activists, radical film makers, aspirant preservers
of dead things in nasty fluids in galleries - imagine this. My parents
wanted to be as MIDDLE CLASS AS POSSIBLE. How unbelievably naff
is that? But I tell you what - if you were born in the Fifties or Sixties,
I bet yours did too. Unless they were already so posh they didn't
need to try!
My mum and dad made it quite a few rungs up the ladder before
he died in 1968: he was a retired civil servant and amateur poet, she
was a housewife and piano teacher, living in a semi-detached near
Brighton, both their hopes of further social advancement resting on
their beloved only son. But sadly for their aspirations, I saw The
Clash in 1977, and from then on the only way I was going on the
ladder was straight back down to the sound of three chords! I didn't
have far to descend: one generational leap and there I was back in
the media-and peer-revered metaphorical council house to which all
Leftie punk rockers aspired.
I know that my mum is, despite certain reservations, thoroughly
proud of her loud, rude, Tory-baiting, Doc Marten–wearing son who
inherited his parents' talent for music and words and earns his living
doing what he loves. I also know that a little bit of her would have
liked me to have continued the route up the ladder and end up a
pinstripe wearing toffy git with a job in the City – a stockbroker, but
minus the Attila.
Sorry Mum. You keep up your appearances. I'll keep up mine!

Beer Gardening

(for all at the Evening Star, Surrey Street, Brighton)

Come into the Beer Garden!
It's not very far.
What's that light that points the way?
It's the Evening Star.
We all love Beer Gardening
As the sun goes down.
Who's that crashed out on the floor?
InCapability Brown.

Come into the Beer Garden
Through the Golden Gate!
Sunburst makes your Hophead swim -
Meltdown seals your fate...
Peas, then Leeks, then Sycamore.
Got to let it go!
What's that in the Yucca Plant?
You don't want to know...

Four hours in the Beer Garden -
God, I need a kip.
Insects are all outsects now.
Flies have got no zip.
Stagger onto the last train.
Cuddle up in bed.
Red Hot Poker's lost his poke.
Shrimp Plant's there instead.

Braintree

On balance, I think,
I'm opposed to genetic modification.
However, this does seem
a very good idea.
Millions would benefit.
After several good harvests
tabloids would fold
television become an underground cult
celebrity an obsolete concept -
spectators, participants.
But we would need so many....
Could your Essex soil sustain such forests?
For we would need forests, huge forests
in this dumbed-down land of ours.
No, sorry, Essex:
we'd have to plant over the border -
Cambridgeshire, perhaps -
and use your natural resources,
your legions of terse, musclebound,
unemployed nightclub bouncers
to guard the precious forests
from Murdoch's scab geneticists
employed, as they surely would be,
to infiltrate late at night
and inject the moron gene back
into the growing fruit.
A grandiose scheme.
A bit ambitious, perhaps.
But it does seem
a wonderful idea.
Let's start off small
and plant just one
in precisely the place in all England
where it is needed the most.
I know.
I used to live there.

We'll set its roots deep
in Harlow town centre
between the Jean Harlow pub,
the disco
and the kebabery
to cast its awesome shadow of wisdom
over testosterone and lager
giving up its heavy, undulating, grey, veiny fruit
to the weekend combatants
so that each and every one
wakes next morning
to The Guardian, Vivaldi and Radio Four.
And The Clash of course.

News would spread fast.
Soon Basildon would have one.
The Lakeside Centre in Thurrock
would sustain a small plantation.
Every shopping mall in England
would put in an order
and soon each would boast one
next to the tasteless water feature.
And then...
Export.
To France?
Home of Sartre and Camus?
I'm sure there would be objections.
A ban, whatever the EU position.
Non!
Danger of infection!
Coals to Newcastle!
But hang on, messieurs-dames:
you have Le Pen,
National Front town councils
and beer so foul
even nitrokeg pales in comparison.
Therefore:
Objection overruled!
From Essex to the world.
The best thing since The Newtown Neurotics,
Wat Tyler
and Ian Dury.
The ultimate genetic modification!
Braintree.

A Hole Series

...of poems for my wife

I love the whole of you.
And all the rest of you.
Not just a part of you.
I love your hole.
Clitorally speaking.
And that's the long, short
and curly of it.

—⁓—

I have a hole in my heart.
I love you
Hole heartedly.

—⁓—

You're feeling tired and stressed.
I find the cure.
Holeistically.

—⁓—

In the bath
Our favourite meal -
Toed in the Hole.

—⁓—

On tour.
What's this?
An envelope
in my mandola case.
'We love you'
it says on the outside.
And inside?

Short curly ones.
Long straight ones.
Now that's what I call
a holeogram!

—⁓—

For a holemeal
We love hole food.
Chocolate spread.
Ice cream.
Finger doughnuts.
But hole grain
is out!

—⁓—

Holesale?
Although rubbish,
on this point at least
the Beatles were right.
Money
can't
buy
you
love.

—⁓—

Driving through West Sussex.
Sign says: 'Crossbush - 1 mile'
Keep us away!
It's got to be a hell hole.
And I can't stand the thought
of a holey war...

For years I'd been aware that my home town had an allegedly more recent namesake, nestling on the tip of the Wirral Peninsula. So during a series of gigs in the Northwest I went on a pilgrimage and afterwards wrote a poem of comparison......

New Brighton

No supercilious yuppie hordes
No rip-off absentee landlords
No crap stude chains to ruin your pub
No overpriced, pretentious grub
No begging crusties hooked on smack
No London dealers pushing crack
No narrow streets clogged up with cars
No endless naff expresso bars
No pissed up blokes who fight and sing
No beer, no life, no...anything!
There IS a fort. Says 'Open'. But
The gates are resolutely shut.
New Brighton. That's a good idea -
But it's not going to happen here...

During a ridiculously long drawn out planning enquiry, the opponents of Brighton and Hove Albion's new football stadium at Falmer were constantly telling us that the site is an Area of Outstanding Natural Beauty - an idyllic village with a beautiful pond. In fact it's bisected by a motorway-sized road, the A27! And as for the pond - one afternoon Robina and I decided to go and have a look at it. It was half dried up, full of noxious algae, and there was a prominent sign – 'Don't feed the ducks, it encourages the rats.' That visit inspired the following poem!

Falmer Pond

Upon approach, the stench of foetid mud.
If, undeterred, you head towards this place
Mosquito clouds fly up into your face:
A vampire squadron, hungry for your blood.
And then you see the rats. Their gimlet eyes
Bore through you, as if sizing up their prey.
But they are full: they have a meal today.
A local dog has just met its demise.
It decomposes while they gnaw its flesh.
Diseased and dying ducks are all around
Choking on the used condoms that they've found
Their scab-encrusted feet caught in a mesh
Of rusting supermarket trolleys. Worse!
A host of bats (protected species, these)
Each carrying a different foul disease
Rises on stinking wings to spread a curse
Across the innocent East Sussex sky.
A chill runs down your spine, the message clear.
Abandon hope, all those who enter here:
This is a place where creatures come to die.
Then, from the shadows, awful shapes lurch forth.
Pale, hideous forms, by putrefaction scarred:
With querulous moans of 'Not In My Back Yard…'
The zombie hordes of Falmer Village North!

Despite the whining, Prescott's word was Yes.
But his advisers made a right old mess
And their mistake gave rise to yet more fears:
At last, the green light thanks to Hazel Blears.
Outstanding Natural Beauty there will be
Next to that awful breeding place for flies.
Not too long now, and we will claim our prize:
A Stadium for the City by the Sea!

Spirit of the Age

You've got to be young and black to rap, right?
So I've no chance 'cos I'm old, punk rock and white...
You've got to be young and black to rap? Wrong!
Anyone can rap - or write a punk rock song
So don't look at me with scorn or derision
I don't accept boundaries of cultural division
I'm MC Attila and I'm right in your face
So listen up folks 'cos I ain't going no place
This rap's called 'Spirit Of The Age'
All my life I'm gonna be on stage
Millions of ideas buzzing round my head
and I'll be rapping till the day I'm dead
Aged 48 I wasn't sedate
Rancid rule, Joe Strummer is my soul mate
49, I was doing just fine
Reeling in the Right on my verbal fishing line
Fifty? I'll be nifty!
So don't look at me like I'm sad or I'm shifty...
51, I'll be having some fun
When Brighton score 10 and Crystal Palace score none
52, I'll be talking to you -
And I'll make more sense than Blink 182...
53? Top of the tree!
Red rebel rhymes and rapping rebel poetry
54, like I said before -
Show me a fascist, I'll show him the floor
55, still cutting it live
While boring arty poets take a nose dive
56, I'll be high in the mix
This old punk rocker will have learned some new tricks
57, still first eleven
Drinking real ale like it's manna from heaven
58, I'll be fuelling debate
Giving it straight from the 51st State
59, laying down the line
Pulling out words and watching them intertwine

60? Still defying convention!
I won't be drawing my punk rock pension...
As long as I'm alive I'll be live on stage:
Age of the spirit - spirit of the age!

Two excerpts from my forthcoming autobiography, 'Arguments Yard'

The Brighton Workers' Bookstore

During the miners' strike of 1972 (three day week, power cuts - some readers will be old enough to remember!) I was sure their cause was right: hearing that pompous git Ted Heath and his upper class cronies whining about the miners 'holding the country to ransom' made me very angry. The Tory government sounded just like the kind of nasty, authoritarian, mean spirited bullies I was up against at school, and I knew that miners were people who did a very dangerous job, earned low pay, and produced the fuel which was the cornerstone of our daily lives. Given that my mum and I had absolutely no money apart from her widow's pension I was naturally on the side of the underdog in any case, and roughly at the same time as the miners' strike there was a terrible murder in a deprived area of Brighton that brought about my earliest attempts to write a directly political poem. Aged about 14 and a half, I resolved to make my first radical contacts, and wandering down Gloucester Road in Brighton one day in my school holidays, I came across something that proclaimed itself in large letters to be 'The Brighton Workers' Bookstore'.

I went inside, and sure enough, there were loads of books. Books by Karl Marx (I'd heard of him!) Lenin (him too) Stalin (him too, but wasn't he supposed to be a bit nasty?) Mao (ah, the Little Red Book, I knew about that) and some bloke called Enver Hoxha (who?) A large pamphlet proudly proclaimed 'Albania – The Only Socialist Country In Europe!' I'd never heard of Albania, and certainly wasn't aware that it was in Europe. I knew a song called 'The Misty Coast of Albany' by Tyrannosaurus Rex, but given Marc Bolan's hippy-bollocks lyrical bent I doubted very much that there was any likelihood of a connection with revolutionary Marxism.

Characteristically, even at that early age, I took the bull by the horns. 'Where's Albania?' I asked the bloke in charge. 'And why is it the only socialist country in Europe? What about Russia and places like that?'

When I walked into that shop I had never heard the word 'revisionist' before. By the time I left, some two hours later, clutching a handful of pamphlets and copies of The Worker

(Weekly Paper of the Communist Party of Britain (Marxist-Leninist)) I had heard the word 'revisionist' many, many times. More times than I would ever have believed possible.

I now knew that Albania stood alone as a beacon of socialism in Europe, and that it was allied to the People's Republic of China. Even if I still didn't know where it was. And I knew that the Soviet Union and its allies were revisionists. Even if – despite listening very hard, and concentrating very hard too – I had, if I am honest, still no idea what 'revisionist' meant.

But I knew it wasn't a nice thing to be.

I went home and got out a map. Soon I knew exactly where Albania was. At the age of 14 and a half, I started to read about Comrade Enver Hoxha, how he led the Albanian communist partisans to victory against the Nazis, and about his battles with the Yugoslav revisionist plotters (if you were a revisionist you were always a plotter - it went with the territory). I started listening to Radio Tirana. And I began to understand the importance of efficient tractor production, something that really hadn't occurred to me before.

Farewell to the Vault

The seismic impact of punk rock had spread quickly all over the country, and by 1977 my hometown had its own thriving scene, based in The Vault. This was, as the name suggested, an old 19th century burial vault, situated in North Road under Brighton Resources Centre, which was the headquarters of the local punk/anarchist/squatter movement. The Vault was simultaneously a rehearsal space and a gig venue, and all the early Brighton punk bands played there. On regular visits home from university to visit my mum and my friends and to watch my beloved Brighton and Hove Albion I had already seen three of Brighton's first bands – Joby & The Hooligans, Wrist Action and the legendary Piranhas (whose legacy I would one day help to revive – but that was nearly 30 years later…) Now it was time to heed Strummer's call and get up there myself. Together with two Albion-supporting mates, Max Cooter (vocals) and Miles Baigent (guitar) we formed Brighton Riot Squad, and tried to find a drummer.

But drummers were in very short supply. Then as now! Even punk drummers were in short supply. You didn't need to be able to play the drums very well, but you still needed to own or have access to a kit. In desperation, we stuck an advert in the local paper, and we got a call from Frank.

Frank claimed to be a drummer, and he did have a kit. He also had that other essential rock 'n' roll prerequisite – a car to drive his kit around in. Hooray! But when we met up for our first rehearsal, our glee was soon tempered by the realisation that having Frank in the band had three major disadvantages.

One: even by the more or less non-existent standards of punk, he couldn't play the drums. A dead turbot had a better sense of rhythm.

Two: he had very dodgy right-wing views: his parents were refugees from somewhere in Eastern Europe, and the very sight of a red flag or the mention of the word 'socialism' made him go nuts.

Three: he was a Teddy Boy.

The rivalry between Teds and punks in 1977 was media-created and of course blown up out of all proportion, but it did exist. Local Teds used to hang about outside the Vault looking for punks to beat up (for the painful results, listen to 'Intensive Care' by Brighton's legendary Peter and the Test Tube Babies) and some punks were happy to return the compliment when the opportunity arose. Soon word of our unorthodox line-up got around, and one of Brighton Riot Squad's rehearsals in the Vault was noisily invaded by another punk band - the very young, very drunk, more or less all girl Molesters. Plus their hangers-on.

'See – I told you! Brighton Riot Squad have a TED DRUMMER! You WANKERS! You should be BEATING HIM UP, not letting him play in your BAND! And where are your BONDAGE TROUSERS? You're wearing FLARES!!! You're HIPPIES!' (For the record: we weren't wearing flares. But we weren't wearing bondage trousers either. We didn't think putting ridiculous amounts of money in Vivienne Westwood's pocket buying overpriced rubbish The Sun told you to wear had much to do with punk rock).

Frank's politics were far more of a problem for us than his dress sense – we liked being different, that was what punk was supposed to be about, and having a Ted drummer certainly was different! Moreover, once we started to practise, we soon realised that what we had perceived to be his biggest drawback of all (the fact that he couldn't play the drums) wasn't going to matter one bit. Max, our singer, was more or less tone deaf. Miles could play the required three chords, but he couldn't get them in the right order much of the time, and I was a complete disaster as a bass player, my self indulgent style totally crap in a punk band. That is in retrospect, of course. I thought the exact opposite at the time…

Somehow, however, we got a set together, or we thought we did: a few of my earliest compositions like 'Your Days Are Numbered' and 'Son of Sam' plus covers of 'Pale Blue Eyes' and 'We're Gonna Have A Real Good Time Together' by the collective heroes of three quarters of the band, the Velvet Underground. (I say three quarters: the fourth member had never heard of them and thought Elvis was The King. I wonder if you can guess which one that was?) Joby Visigoth of Joby & The Hooligans designed a great poster for us. 'BRIGHTON…RIOT SQUAD!' it proclaimed at the top, above a large and brilliantly executed drawing of a riot policeman, truncheon raised menacingly above his head. We booked the Vault, plastered posters all over Brighton, and waited with bated breath for our first gig. I asked Vi Subversa of the legendary Poison Girls, who at the time were based in Brighton, if we could use their PA system. 'As long as nothing gets broken!' she eventually agreed, with an understandable mixture of reluctance and suspicion.

The big day came. The Vault was packed: our posters really did look good, and we had plastered them everywhere. Joby & The Hooligans supported us, and they were really good, too.

We weren't. We were absolutely awful.

We were worse than Crystal Palace.

(If you don't understand the utterly, terminally damning nature of this statement, you will when you've read the football chapter).

We didn't manage to get the required three chords in the right order very much, and, thanks to Frank, were also completely out of time with each other. But we stuck to our guns and carried on. Vi Subversa stood at the front all the way through our set like a concerned mother hen, worried that the crowd were going to attack us – and therefore her PA - because we were so crap. But Vi needn't have worried. It was a punk rock gig: the crowd were used to seeing bands that couldn't play, and they didn't attack us. Rather the opposite, in fact. They paid us the ultimate mid-1977 punk rock compliment.

They gobbed at us from start to finish.

That was our one and only gig, which itself is pretty punk rock, I reckon. I'm still friendly with both Max and Miles, nearly 30 years later. As for Frank – he's probably an Elvis impersonator. In Hungary. I'm sure his parents came from Hungary.

Wherever he is, I doubt very much that he's a drummer...

It won't surprise you to learn that the local emergent punk scene managed to survive the demise of Brighton Riot Squad: it went from strength to strength (The Depressions, Nicky & the Dots, Devil's Dykes, Peter & the Test Tube Babies, The Dodgems, Smeggy & the Cheesy Bits... to name but a few of the other early bands) and on my visits home from university I turned up at the gigs whenever I could and sometimes helped out on the door or by putting up posters. But there was a developing problem. Before the punks had been let loose there, walls had been constructed in front of the actual burial chambers: the vibrations from rehearsals and gigs, plus general vandalism, caused breaches in them, and pretty soon skulls, bones and bits of coffin started turning up. Someone arrived at a gig with a skull they had found in a local telephone box.

Then whole coffins started to appear with still legible inscriptions, many with French names and plaques dating from the mid 1800s. Hugenot refugees, some having succumbed to some kind of plague - I distinctly remember one inscription 'victime de la peste'. This worried me! One evening I had volunteered to take the money on the door and on arrival the first thing I saw was a little baby's lead coffin, about a foot long, with the bones still inside. With due deference I moved the bones to one end and used the rest as a cashbox. If all this had happened ten years later I guess the Vault would have become the most popular Goth or death metal venue in the world – surely this was the very definition of death metal, or at the very least death punk - but there weren't any Goths or death metallers then and many of us were actually rather uneasy about the whole thing. Not just because it seemed a bit disrespectful: I remember sitting in the Three Jolly Butchers over the road having a discussion about exactly how long a plague bacillus could survive…!

Eventually, with skeletons quite literally coming out of the closet all the time, as it were, things got too much: the local council took action and the Vault's doors closed for good. When a 'mysterious' (fascist-perpetrated) fire burned down the Resources Centre above, that colourful chapter in Brighton's musical history came to an end, though it is preserved for posterity on two compilation albums, 'Vaultage 78' and 'Vaultage 79' on Brighton's seminal Attrix record label.

SONG LYRICS

Guy Fawkes' Table

I wrote this song in the Mother Shipton Inn, Knaresborough, North Yorkshire, on the day Blair's government voted to support Bush's illegal war in Iraq. I was on tour in the North of England and had gone to Knaresborough because it is a very historic town, a famous English Civil War site and the birthplace of Guy Fawkes (for non UK readers, he was the man behind the Gunpowder Plot of 1605, when a group of Catholic zealots tried to blow up the Houses of Parliament). Sitting in that pub I noticed a plaque on the - very old - table next to my pint.
'This table belonged to Guy Fawkes' it said...'

'Guy Fawkes' Table' was written in the next twenty minutes.

I'm sitting at Guy Fawkes' table
The day Parliament voted for war
Though the mass of the people oppose it
And it flouts international law
I'm sitting at Guy Fawkes' table
While American thugs flaunt their power
Egged on by a sad little muppet
And his craven and cowardly shower.

CHORUS

Aneurin Bevan, your party is dead
And the time for a new one is nigh
Will the last person Left please turn out the lights?
New Labour, just fuck off and die.

They won't be caught up in the carnage
They'll be pontificating right here
Their kids won't be Iraqi conscripts
Moved down while they're shitting with fear
Saddam was the Yanks' chosen ally
On a whim, they now say he must fall
So they'll carpet bomb defenceless soldiers -
But that's not 'mass destruction' at all...

CHORUS

I'm sitting at Guy Fawkes' table
As Bush and his muppet connive
And I'm filled with unprintable anger
And I'm thinking of 1605
One message, Dishonourable Members
Who endorsed an illegal attack -
No, I don't want to bomb you like Guy did
But I'd love to send you to Iraq.

CHORUS

We need a new socialist party -
But not the Judean People's Front
Not another small sect, but a movement
With the power to change and confront
We need an electoral system
Which gives every voter a voice
Cos we're fed up with voting for traitors
And we have the right to a choice!

CHORUS

Death of a Salesman

(written just after the attacks on the World Trade Centre)

You were there in Chile, 11 September '73
Twenty eight years to the day - what a dreadful irony
Victor Jara singing 'midst the tortured and the dead
White House glasses clinking as Allende's comrades bled

You were there in '79 in the hills above Kabul
Teaching a bunch of psychopaths the fastest way to kill
Just pawns in your global strategy, another little right wing war
But now you reap just what you sow - the monster's at the door

CHORUS

And you don't understand why those people are so angry
And you don't understand why they don't go shopping too
And you don't understand why your garish colours blind them
Dismiss, exploit and bully - then you wonder at their hate
So many cruel deaths
But these are different, these are American
Now death counts - death of a salesman

You use the world as your sweatshop on a bare subsistence wage
Then along come medieval murderers to exploit the people's rage
And Europe takes the profits too, then grovels on its knees
Saying 'after you, you rule the world, so do just as you please'

CHORUS

And you don't understand why those people are so hungry
And you don't understand why they can't go shopping too
And you don't understand why your garish colours blind them
Dismiss, exploit and bully - then you wonder at their hate
So many cruel deaths
But these are different, these are American
Now death counts - death of a salesman

We don't need your religion, whether Allah, money or God
We won't cheer on your armies, won't wield your avenging rod
We stand for justice, for the future,
for the millions of women and men
Who see through the lies and work for the day
when sanity rules again

CHORUS

Hey Celebrity

CHORUS

Hey celebrity! TV bore!
What have you done to be famous for?
Hey celebrity! Tabloid whore!
What do people need you for...?

Once again the headlines shout
I don't know what they're on about
I've got my own life, don't need yours
Use TV for the teletext scores
Why do they need you, what do they see?
I don't need you, I'm happy with me
Millions and millions of women and men
Watching you again and again
Talking about you, again and again
Living through you, again and again...

CHORUS

Brain dead TV soap, Big Brother
Shepherds for the sheep one way or the other
Celebrity diet, celebrity dress
Celebrity trivia, celebrity press
One day one of you said to me
'Hey, Attila, that's how you want to be
All your talk's just jealousy
You just want to be like me
You just want to live like me
Want to be famous just like me
Want to be famous just like me...'

CHORUS

Why do they all want this stuff?
Why aren't their own lives more than enough?
We've so much to see and do
We've no time to waste on you...
Hardly ever watch TV
Read the news selectively
You're on telly, in the tabloids too
We're not interested in you
We're not interested in you
We're not interested in you
We're not interested in you...

CHORUS

Comandante Joe

(Dedicated to the memory of Joe Strummer, 1952-2002)

I guess in quite a lot of ways I grew up just like you
A bolshy kid who didn't think the way they told him to
You kicked over the statues, a roots rock rebel star
Who knew that punk was more than just the sound of a guitar
And I'll always remember that night at the Rainbow
When you wrote a soundtrack for my life,
Comandante Joe.

So many bands back then were like too many bands today
A bunch of blokes who made a noise with bugger all to say
The Clash were always out in front, you put the rest to shame
Your words were calls to action, your music was a flame
You were our common Dante, and you raised an inferno
And you wrote a soundtrack for my life,
Comandante Joe.

Reggae in the Palais
Midnight till six!
Rockin' Reds in Brockwell Park!
Sten guns in Knightsbridge!
Up and down the Westway
In and out the lights!
Clash City Rockers!
Know Your Rights!

I guess in quite a lot of ways I grew up just like you
A bolshy kid who didn't think the way they told him to
Like you I always knew that words and music held the key
As you did for so many, you showed the way to me
Although I never met you, I'm so sad to see you go
Cos you wrote a soundtrack for my life,
Comandante Joe.

An anti-fascist T.Rex number – dedicated to Marc, written by me in the musical style of T.Rex. A song about the injustice of the human condition!

Scumball Pinochet

One wrote songs that meant a lot to me
but his partner wrapped a Mini round a sycamore tree
and the other one was evil fascist torturing scum
but he lived to over ninety – the Reaper wouldn't come

CHORUS

*Scumball Pinochet should have got a ricochet
20th Century Boy should still be getting it on today (x2)*

One met his Metal Guru at the age of twenty nine
While the other one grew old on torture and wine
It's sixty years too short and it's eighty years too long
and the Children Of The Revolution think it's wrong!

CHORUS

They both had their heyday in 1973
One was The Groover who Loved To Boogie
The other killed thousands of people in Chile
And he lived to be old – that's really bloody silly...

And the message from the government's the really last Straw
that a killer aged eighty's not a killer any more
But one way or another he's gone to meet his fate
And Telegram Sam says hell can't wait!

CHORUS

Only Football

His forebears were the butchers on the field at Peterloo
They led the charge and cut the people down
They ruled the mill, starved weavers out,
beat Chartists black and blue
Made millions in some hellish sweatshop town
I'm sure he cursed his countrymen in '84 and '5
His queen called them 'the enemy within'
He's the overseer, the usurer, drone within the hive
Whose wallet is his god, his kith and kin

and don't tell me it's only football

His system defines 'ownership' – a mess of paper shares
A slick deal, a commodity acquired
He pulls the strings and works the law so he controls the 'wares'
Then laughs at all the anguish he's inspired
Now we are many thousands, and he is only one
But law and state hold him in their embrace
What kind of law, what kind of state condones what he has done?
A state where social justice has no place

CHORUS

*So don't tell me it's only football
And above all, friends, don't tell me please
That it's nothing to do with years of sleaze
The shattered lives and the corporate trough
Don't tell me it's just a sad one-off
That it's nothing to do with politics
That politics and sport don't mix
Don't tell me it's just bad luck
And don't tell me it's only football*

Our grounds rose up near stations in old Victorian times
Most urban centres then were barely towns
Built for our teams, then left in trust to us across the years
By people who loved football, not just pounds
The vulture sees the soaring price of inner city land
An ailing club which he can desecrate
To us it's pride and history, the story of our lives
To him it's just some prime site real estate

CHORUS

Our culture has been colonised, our heritage is sold
And moneymen control our national game
It's devil take the hindmost, all hail the Premier League
And if you can't compete, well, that's a shame
There's a superstore development and it's coming to your ground
A pinstriped butcher's waiting with his knife
Brighton, Wrexham, anywhere, the lesson is the same
Let's kick him out – of football, and of life!

CHORUS

I'd like to think that the chorus of this song may one day make its way into the opposing fans' repertoire when they are playing the Chelski mercenaries...

Abramovich's Donkey Sanctuary

Most of the time you'll find these places quietly tucked away
Run by a bunch of crusties or the RSPCA
But when you see the latest one I'm sure you will agree
That every creature in it has a Premier pedigree...
It's funded by the billions leeched by private profiteers
From Soviet oil resources built up over the years
So take a walk to Stamford Bridge and soon you'll plainly see
The universe's most exclusive donkey sanctuary!

CHORUS

Donkey sanctuary, donkey sanctuary
Hey Mr Abramovich, will you buy one from me?
Donkey sanctuary, donkey sanctuary
They're overpriced, they're over here, they're playing for Chelsea!

He wants a new one every day so he puts in a bid
And each new one costs double the amount the last one did
That's twenty times more than they would have cost a week ago
The Price is Right for Roman however high you go
And all the while most of our clubs are fighting to survive
With buckets and collections just to help them stay alive
Some call this 'market forces' but we call it right wing shit
In football, and in life, we've had far too much of it!

CHORUS

So hate Man U for ever - but hate Chelsea even more
Phone up Stamford Bridge and ask 'What's Russian for Ee-aw?'
Rejoice each time they lose a game, abuse them when they win
Cos they're a plastic football club, a profiteer's plaything
That money is the people's cash - in Russia it should stay
A curse upon the traitors who gave Soviet wealth away
A few clubs get the millions, the rest go to the wall
So let's kick out the profiteers - and let's take back the ball!

CHORUS

Baghdad Ska

Hooray Hooray for the USA!
Your soldiers took Saddam away
So we're all going out on the streets to play
And celebrate our liberation day
The hospitals overflow with dead
The looters have stolen all the bread
But I think my family are all OK
and you said this was the only way
You said this was the only way...
I saw an old friend the very next day
Armed to the teeth and up for the fray
He said 'I'll make those Yankees pay!'
- A B52 blew his wife away
I put my hand upon his head
I held him close and softly said
'I know it's an awful price to pay'...
Then sadly I went on my way
Sadly I went on my way

CHORUS
This is Baghdad's scar
This is Baghdad ska
This is Baghdad's scar
This is Baghdad ska...

Walked up to a Yankee the other day
Asked how long they were going to stay
And how he'd reply to the folks who say
Our land was stolen by the USA
Then a shot rang out from across the road
I stood and watched his head explode
And all I could do was cringe and pray
As boots and fists took me away
Boots and fists took me away

CHORUS

They're gonna take me to Guantanamo Bay
An enemy of the USA
They don't believe a word I say
They sneer that I'm in for a very long stay
I cry my own, my country's tears
How many dead, how many years?
And in my agony I say:
there could have been another way...

CHORUS

Bunter's Revolution

For the Countryside Alliance

The cabbage millions get their fix in front of the TV
as the camera shifts to the trucker boys at the oil refinery
While farmers drive their tractors in convoys round the square
and Middle England yawns approval from his favourite chair
and Middle England yawns approval from his favourite chair.

No more those good old striking days, no more those days of rage.
It's second hand rebellion - TV, the tabloid page...
No more the red flag at the helm, the altruistic fight:
It's PETROL DOWN and HANG THE FOX, the slogans of the Right
It's PETROL DOWN and HANG THE FOX, the slogans of the Right.

Cos greed is good, the word is out, and Bunter's got the call.
He's holding up his banner and it says 'I want it all!'
His postal order's finally come, and so's his credit card
But he's as green as green can be - he eats unleaded lard.
But he's as green as green can be - he eats unleaded lard.

Let's take the truckers off the road, put freight back on the rails.
Let's blood the Tally Ho brigade with Jeffrey Archer's tales...
Renationalise the railways, defend our local shops.
Put farmers on collective farms and make them all grow hops!
Put farmers on collective farms and make them all grow hops!

Song For The Defeated

Your dreams are gone, but your life goes on
And you're happy in your day to day
In your middle age, at the end of rage,
we meet and we've nothing to say

CHORUS
And you shake my hand, but your eyes show your disdain
So sad, so bland - I know we'll never meet again

In your fiery youth, when you spoke the truth
I believed you and called you my friend
But the winds of change blow wild and strange
and with sadness I watched you bend

CHORUS

You serve those whom you vowed you would never serve
You take from those with nothing to give
Those days in '89 were the end of the line
And now you just say live and let live
I knew that it would never be easy
But I never thought you'd swallow that lie
Because live and let live for the likes of us
For some means live and let die
And the bond
is broken now...

You have made your peace, you have have found release
but your peace is the still of the dead
'a misguided phase' - what an empty phrase
to pour scorn on the life you once led

CHORUS

Valentine's Day

(Another true story)

I said come, we'll make it special, and here we are, Valentine's Day
In a wild impetuous journey up the M1 motorway
In my boots and Rancid sweatshirt I'll try hard to cut a dash
And I'll serenade you, darling, with Hans Blix and the Clash

Now you say I'm not romantic, but you know I can beguile
That daffodil was dead - but oh, presented with such style!
A bindweed flower buttonhole, some earrings with panache
And hours and hours of traffic jams with Hans Blix and the Clash

There's war news on the radio
Joe Strummer on the stereo
And something happening down below
That no-one else can see
Another town, another show
But always I need you to know
You make me think and make me grow
The other half of me

Here's to us, our great adventure, and to you, my darling wife
I will stand so proud beside you through the ups and downs of life
As your fingers do the walking I will try hard not to crash
And I'll bring us safe to Sheffield with Hans Blix and The Clash...

Twenty Years

(Written at the turn of the millennium)

I look back on the years before, it's half a lifetime now
Hilare Belloc, and my father, and a small size violin
Then the pain of death, and parting: those awful preteen days
Till the time I picked the ball up and took them all on - on my own
Then I came through, and I punched the air the day I left that place
And it freed the words and music, though I wasn't quite sure how
Then I saw four men on a London stage who were playing just for me
And I walked out of the Rainbow, and I knew just what to do.

'77 was year zero, and me, I was nineteen
I played the bass, and wrote the words, but I wanted something more
So I travelled, and I played the bass, then I put the bass away
And I wrote the words, and blagged a gig,
and got up there on my own
And I felt the people understand, though this was something new
When Peel played my first record I thought: 'Bloody hell, that's me!'
And Clarkie, Zephaniah, Joolz, Swells and me were that year's thing
And I said 'Thanks Joe' as Gordon Smith
took Robbo's crossfield pass...

Twenty years.

But Gordon missed, and Thatcher ruled,
and Warhol's words came true
I was writing all my best stuff, but the music press said 'Crap!'
I can't say it didn't hurt, but I am confident and strong
Once again I picked the ball up and took them all on - on my own
I was writing for the people I saw fighting for their lives
At Orgreave and at Wapping, at Greenham and Brick Lane
Not for journalists or telly, but for justice and for truth
And I played for all the people who felt just the same as me...

And I toured across East Germany before the Wall came down
Saw hope, dreams and intelligence, frustration and despair
Through Europe, then to Canada, across it, coast to coast
New Zealand and Australia - that huge, mystical land

And I played for all the people who felt just the same as me
(And I argued with the others cos I knew that I was right!)
Then I came home, cos it is home, though the Tories had its soul
And I played for all the people who felt just the same as me

Twenty years.

We fought to save the Albion - I still want to change the world
And the day that Hove went Labour I thought we might have a chance
Now we know that it was all a con - there must be something more
And I wrote this for the people who feel just the same as me...
Cos I still feel all the things I felt when I first saw the Clash
That belief, that inspiration - I'm not mellowing with age
And when someone says 'You still going? I saw you in '82!'
I smile and say: 'Now let me guess - you read the NME... '

And I still wake up at 2 am and have to write a song
And I still rage at injustice and believe that things can change
And I cherish all the people who feel just the same as me
And I thank you, cos it's down to you that I can live this way
Looking forward to the future as I celebrate the past
I remember how I picked it up and ran through on my own
And I hold her and we watch him as he charges for the line
He's a far, far better player, but he's just the same as me...

Twenty years.

...and that one's for Joe.